First World War
and Army of Occupation
War Diary
France, Belgium and Germany

58 DIVISION
175 Infantry Brigade
17 March 1917 - 28 February 1918

WO95/3009/12

The Naval & Military Press Ltd
www.nmarchive.com
Published in association with The National Archives

Published by

The Naval & Military Press Ltd

Unit 10 Ridgewood Industrial Park,

Uckfield, East Sussex,

TN22 5QE England

Tel: +44 (0) 1825 749494

www.naval-military-press.com

www.nmarchive.com

This diary has been reprinted in facsimile from the original. Any imperfections are inevitably reproduced and the quality may fall short of modern type and cartographic standards.

© Crown Copyright
Images reproduced by permission of The National Archives, London, England, 2015.

Contents

Document type	Place/Title	Date From	Date To
Heading	WO95/3009/11 (Apr 1917 Missing)		
Heading	58th Division 175th Division 215th Machine Gun Coy. Mar 1917-Feb 1918		
War Diary	Havre	17/03/1917	19/03/1917
War Diary	Doullens	20/03/1917	21/03/1917
War Diary	Lacauchie	21/03/1917	22/03/1917
War Diary	La Bazeque Farm	22/03/1917	25/03/1917
War Diary	Beaurepaire	25/03/1917	31/03/1917
War Diary	Achiet Le Petit	01/05/1917	04/05/1917
War Diary	Favreul	05/05/1917	06/05/1917
War Diary	Line	07/05/1917	15/05/1917
War Diary	Bihucourt	16/05/1917	19/05/1917
War Diary	Line	20/05/1917	31/05/1917
Heading	War Diary Of 215 M.G. Coy From 1/6/17 To 30/6/17		
War Diary	Mory	01/06/1917	04/06/1917
War Diary	In The Line	05/06/1917	15/06/1917
War Diary	Mory	16/06/1917	24/06/1917
War Diary	Logeast Wood	25/06/1917	30/06/1917
Miscellaneous	To 58th Divisional Headquarters From Q.C. 215 M.G. Company,		
War Diary	Berneville	01/08/1917	31/08/1917
Miscellaneous	To Headquarters 58th Division From Q.C 175th Infantry Brigade		
War Diary	Line	01/09/1917	12/09/1917
War Diary	Reigersberg Camp	12/09/1917	12/09/1917
War Diary	Brake Camp	13/09/1917	18/09/1917
War Diary	Line	19/09/1917	28/09/1917
War Diary	Reigersberg Camp	28/09/1917	28/09/1917
War Diary	Rambre Camp	29/09/1917	30/09/1917
Miscellaneous	To Headquarters 58th Division From Q.C. 215 M.G Company		
War Diary	Brake Camp	01/10/1917	01/10/1917
War Diary	Bertham	02/10/1917	21/10/1917
War Diary	Road Camp St Jan Ter Biezen	22/10/1917	31/10/1917
Miscellaneous	QE 3.56		
Miscellaneous	To 58th Division From Q.C. 215 M.G Company		
War Diary		01/11/1917	09/11/1917
War Diary	Siege Camp	10/11/1917	14/11/1917
War Diary	Point Camp	15/11/1917	27/11/1917
War Diary	Affringue	28/11/1917	30/11/1917
War Diary	Lart	01/12/1917	06/12/1917
War Diary	Siege Camp	07/12/1917	08/12/1917
War Diary	In The Line	09/12/1917	12/12/1917
War Diary	Canal Bank	13/12/1917	14/12/1917
War Diary	Roussel Camp	15/12/1917	22/12/1917
War Diary	Canal Bank	23/12/1917	23/12/1917
War Diary	Line	24/12/1917	31/12/1917
War Diary	Canal Bank	01/01/1918	06/01/1918
War Diary	Houtkerque	07/01/1918	21/01/1918
War Diary	Aubigny	22/01/1918	31/01/1918

Miscellaneous	To 58th Division From Q.C 215 M.G Company			
War Diary	Aubigny		01/02/1918	07/02/1918
War Diary	Line		08/02/1918	28/02/1918

WO 95 3009/11

(Apr 1917 missing)

58TH DIVISION
175TH DIVISION

215TH MACHINE GUN COY.
MAR 1917-FEB 1918

WAR DIARY
or
INTELLIGENCE SUMMARY.

(Erase heading not required.)

Army Form C. 2118.

215 COMPANY MACHINE GUN CORPS

Place	Date	Hour	Summary of Events and Information	Remarks and references to Appendices
HAVRE	17.3.17	1.30 p.m.	The Company disembarked. Fine day.	ADD
"	18.3.17	2 A.m.	Arrived at No 2 Rest Camp.	ADD
"	19.3.17	10.30 p.m.	Left No 2 Rest Camp. Entrained at Point 6, Highland train.	ADD
DOULLENS	20.3.17	7 p.m.	Detrained. Spent the night at Rest Camp near Station. Snow & occasional sleet	ADD
"	21.3.17	10 A.m.	Left DOULLENS (by road) Cold wind.	ADD
LACAUCHIE	"	3 p.m.	Arrived at LA CAUCHIE and billeted there. Joined the 58th (LONDON) Division. 175th Infantry Brigade.	ADD
"	22.3.17	11.6.m.	Left LA CAUCHIE and marched to — Very cold.	
LABARZQUE FARM.	"	12.30 p.m.	Where the Company was billeted in huts.	ADD

WAR DIARY
or
INTELLIGENCE SUMMARY.
(Erase heading not required.)

Army Form C. 2118.

Place	Date	Hour	Summary of Events and Information	Remarks and references to Appendices
LA BAZÈQUE FARM.	23.3.17	—	Spent the day in cleaning up and checking guns, spare parts etc. Occasional snow & sleet storms.	ADD
"	24.3.17	9-12 n.n.	Practice in the use of pack saddlery for the purpose of the carrying guns & ammunition.	ADD
"	"	2-4	All Officers N.C.O's & men were fitted with a small box respirator and went through a gas chamber with them on. Summer time came into force. Cold wind & hail.	
"	25.3.17	4 p.m.	The Company marched from LA BAZÈQUE FARM. On the road orders were received for three sections to proceed to KAGLN, FOSSEUX & GOUY for antiaircraft defence, on the 26th s.m. Nos 2, 3 & 4 sections respectively were detailed marching to LA BAZÈQUE FARM. No 1 Section & Headqrs. altern proceeded	

WAR DIARY
or
INTELLIGENCE SUMMARY.

Army Form C. 2118.

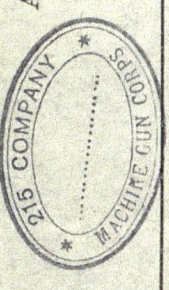

Place	Date	Hour	Summary of Events and Information	Remarks and references to Appendices
BEAUREPAIRE	25.3.17	1.30	To BEAUREPAIRE arriving at 1.30 p.m. Cold wind and hot fine.	ADD
"	26.3.17	9-12 2-4	No 1 Section. Preliminary work on gun.	
			The three sections at SAULTY, FOSSEUX & GOUY reported satisfactorily from 64th M.G.C. at 12 noon. No enemy aircraft seen. Very cold wind	ADD
"	27.3.17	9-12 2-4	No 1 Section. Packsaddle drill. Arms drill. Gas drill.	
			The anti-aircraft sections reported everything quiet. The O.C. went round all three sections. The Company was hard at it. Cold wind and snow showers.	ADD

WAR DIARY
or
INTELLIGENCE SUMMARY.
(Erase heading not required.)

Army Form C. 2118.

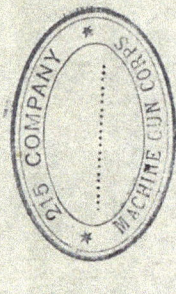

Place	Date	Hour	Summary of Events and Information	Remarks and references to Appendices
BEAUREPAIRE	21 K 30	9-12 2-1.m	No. 9 Section continued training. The anti-aircraft sections reported no enemy aircraft seen. Fairly fine day.	A.D.D.
"	29.3.17		No. 1 Section took part in scheme attended by G.O.C. Machine gun officers. The anti-aircraft sections were relieved at 12 noon by 206 Co. M.G.C. and arrived at BEAUREPAIRE between 6 - 8 p.m. Cold wet day.	A.D.D.
"	30.3.17	a.m 10.30 p.m	Coy hang together. C. spent rest of day in cleaning guns limbers etc. Officers went on scheme with Corps M.G.O. Showery	A.D.D.

WAR DIARY
or
INTELLIGENCE SUMMARY.

Army Form C. 2118.

Place	Date	Hour	Summary of Events and Information	Remarks and references to Appendices
BEAUFETARE	31/3/17		Nothing of interior occurring. In the afternoon the G.O.C 175 Inf. Bde. inspected the company. Showery	ADD

WAR DIARY of 215 M.G. Coy.

Army Form C. 2118.

Month: MAY

Place	Date	Hour	Summary of Events and Information	Remarks and references to Appendices
ACHIET.LE.PETIT. MAY	1st	3 P.M.	Company inspected by Medical Officer. Half Company inoculated T.A.B. (FINE)	
	2nd		Remainder of Company inoculated T.A.B. Training comprised M.G. signals Stripping O.E. (FINE)	
	3rd		Demonstration before staff of M.G. fire-power as compared with rifle & Lewis Gun. (FINE)	
	4th	1.45 P.M.	The Company proceeded by march route to canvas camp near FAVREUIL. (FINE)	
FAVREUIL	5th	2.30 P.M.	The Company proceeded to the line in LAGNICOURT Sector to relieve 2nd Australian M.G.Co.	
	6	2 A.M.	Relief completed. Positions viz:- Support line, Company H.Q. & Nos 3 & 4 sections. Front line Nos 1 & 2 section. Company Transport remained at FAVREUIL. Rear Coy H.Q. at BOIS DE MARICOURT.	
		8 A.M.	Two casualties Nº1 Section. 1 Corporal 1 Private. remainder of day quiet. (FINE)	
LINE	7	6mn to 1am	Situation quiet. 3 M.G.s fired on Enemy Front Support trenches in cooperation with Artillery 9.30 P.M. from Zero + 2 to Zero + 6 in front of QUEANT. 3000 rounds fired (FINE)	HAR. 9/1000 57c N.W 9/1000 57c N.E 19/1000
	8	6am to 1am	Situation quiet. Between 10 p.m and 12 midnight one M.G. fired on C.24.d. 7.7 and rounds in D.7.C 40.0 & D.7.C 70.30	
	9	4am to 5am	Nº1 section relieved by Nº3 section in right sub-section. Nº2 section relieved by Nº4 in left sub-section.	
	10	12 MN to 2 AM	Relief completed: 2 Guns of 14th Australian M.G.Co relieved two guns and one subsection of Nº2 section in nauve. Making 10 guns in forward positions and 4 in reserve.	
	11	1.30 A.M. to 1.5 AM	Company relieved by 8th Australian M.G.Co. Relief completed. On completion of relief company took up positions in reserve line MORCHIES-YTRES line 9 cms 1.2 inch.	

Instructions regarding War Diaries and Intelligence Summaries are contained in F. S. Regs., Part II. and the Staff Manual respectively. Title pages will be prepared in manuscript.

WAR DIARY
or
INTELLIGENCE SUMMARY.
(Erase heading not required.)

215 COMPANY 31/5/17 MACHINE GUN CORPS

Army Form C. 2118.

Place	Date MAY	Hour	Summary of Events and Information	Remarks and references to Appendices
	12th	2 PM.	The Company less transport moved into canvas camp at FAVRUEL. (FINE)	OBY
	13.	AM PM 9 - 4	Inspections:- Clothing, Iron Rations, Gas appliances (FINE)	OBY
	14.	AM. Noon 9 - 12	do. do. do. do. (FINE)	OBY
	15	2 PM.	Company transport joined and moved with company to BIHUCOURT. Company took over part of Australian Canvas Camp. (FINE.)	OBY
BIHUCOURT.	16.	AM Noon 10 - 12.	Lectures to sections re work in trenches. (RAINING)	OBY
-do-	17.	AM. PM 9 - 3	Physical training. Gas drill. Arms drill. Immediate Action. FINE.	OBY
-do-	18.		Brigade Gas demonstration: Baths:	OBY
	19	2 PM.	Company marched to camp at VRAUCOURT. About B. 30 a 0. 0	
		8.00 PM	The Company relieved 206 M.G. Co. in the HINDENBURG-LINE. East of BULLECOURT.	57.C. 1/40000. OBY
LINE.	20	4 AM	(Relief complete. Positions viz:- No 3 section & one subsection of No 4 section took over positions in front & Support line Right Subsector No 1 Section and one subsection of No 4 section took up positions in Railway embankment at C.4.b. & C.5.a. No 2 section in reserve in C.10.c. Company H.Q. in Railway embankment:	Ecoust St Mein U.1.D 2/1/20000 OBY
do	20.		Quiet day, intermittent shelling. (FINE.)	
	21.	AM 3-10	174th Brigade attacked on our left BOVIS-TRENCH. One Gun No 3 section brought fire to bear on U.22.A from front line about 750 rounds fired. Two guns on left of support line were ready to fire in case of emergency. During Counter Barrage by enemy Lieut Wright O/C No 4 Section was killed. Remainder of day quiet. (FINE)	OBY

A5834 Wt. W4973 M687 750,000 8/16 D. D. & L. Ltd. Forms/C.2118/13.

WAR DIARY
or
INTELLIGENCE SUMMARY.
(Erase heading not required.)

Army Form C. 2118.

Instructions regarding War Diaries and Intelligence Summaries are contained in F. S. Regs., Part II. and the Staff Manual respectively. Title pages will be prepared in manuscript.

215 COMPANY MACHINE GUN CORPS 3/5/17

Place	Date MAY.	Hour	Summary of Events and Information	Remarks and references to Appendices
LINE	22nd		Two guns of No 3 Section withdrawn to support line from left forward position. Day Quiet. 1 hospital and 1 private wounded.	MGY
	23rd		No 2 Section relieved No 3 Section in front line;- 2 guns No 1 section relieved 2 guns No 4 sec. 2 guns No 4 withdrawn from Railway Embankment and placed in reserve position on NOREUIL - LONGATTE Road. Quiet day. FINE.	MGY
	24th		Quiet day intermittent shelling. M.G. fired on Roads and approaches to HENDICOURT during night. One private wounded while carrying rations. THUNDERY.	MGY
	25th		Quiet day. Nothing of importance to record. FINE.	MGY
	26th		Quiet day. 2 guns of No 3 Section withdrawn from reserve and taken back to transport lines. Intermittent shelling. Quiet- FINE.	MGY
	27th		Quiet day. Company relieved by 198 M.G. Co. and one gun of 21m m.g. C. Relief complete.	MGY
	28th	A.M. 1.30	Company returned to Transport lines till 2 P.M. 29th inst- Company less Transport moved to canvas camp near MORY.	MGY
	29th			MGY
	30th	A.M. A.M. 9 & 3	Cleaning limbers. Inspection Gas appliances Gas Return clothing etc.	MGY
	31.		Physical Training Belt filling:	MGY

Confidential Vol 4

Way Jun
Ris M Gilson 16/1/17
given 16/1/17
4 16/1/17

WAR DIARY
or
INTELLIGENCE SUMMARY.
(Erase heading not required.)

Army Form C. 2118.

Place	Date	Hour	Summary of Events and Information	Remarks and references to Appendices
MORY	June 1		Physical Drill. Immediate Action. Gun Drill. Barks	Fine
	2		Physical Drill. Arms Drill. Immediate Action. M.G. Aymers Care & cleaning	Fine
	3		Church Parade	Fine
	4		Physical Training. Cleaning. Packing Limbers. Checking spare parts	Fine
	5		Company took over line from 198 M.G. Coy. 5 guns under Lt Carpenter 15th m/g position in advance posts. 1h &. Sau took up positions in support line. one gun on extreme right under 2/Lt Heap in front line. 2 guns under 2/Lt Brown in the gun pits authorised	Fine
	6		No 4 Gun taken to rear position where game support fired 5 times on to BOIS TRENER. Alternative position also made for No 1 Gun. No 7 Gun did indirect fire from C.5 L.33 on C. dumps at U.22.L.45. 400 rounds fired 5.00 p.m.	Fine
	7		Our emplacements in front line received attention from enemy's T.M.'s about 10.30 P.M. N.G. did not fire during the night owing to infantry patrols being at work. About 11.30 P.M. it was reported that our 1st line infantry dropped a past into the line. A working party of about 60 men were dispersed with some casualties by No 1 gun 4mm. While working on supposed T.M. emplacement.	Fine
	8		No 7 Gun at intermediate fired on U.14 A.3 about 400 rounds. 200 rounds fired at enemy aircraft. Fairly quiet day intermittent shelling of BARS during later part	Fine
	9		Gun positions unsuccessfully visited by C.O. 2/10 Batt and continued very quiet day nothing of importance took place	Fine
	10		Fairly quiet day enemy started support line higher at intervals but to no effect. At 11 PM information was received that enemy were moving about U.23 a.c. 1 Gun [illegible] immediately, opened into position and 100 rounds were fired with effect. that movement ceased. At 12.15 AM. 5 gun of a brigade fire. No 3 Gun of No 4 section was relieved at 12.45 AM by a team from No 1 section.	Fine

WAR DIARY
INTELLIGENCE SUMMARY
(Erase heading not required.)

Army Form C. 2118.

Place	Date	Hour	Summary of Events and Information	Remarks and references to Appendices
In the line	June 11 1917		Gun in entanglement found at U.24.a.1.9 at 8.20pm on early ration party of the enemy about 250 rounds fired. Three teams destroyed by Sgt M²² then about 12.45 AM relieved teams proceeded to transport lines. Very quiet day, enemy movement considerable during early hours of morning on ridge between RIENCOURT and HENDICOURT. No movement in BOVIS TRENCH observed but many lights sent up from U.22 c.0.5. during the night	True
	12		About 350 rounds fired at enemy aircraft 3.50 PM. She came at once with two bombs where it appeared to make for a landing. At 8.50 PM transport was heard very audibly about U.24.c.1.9, a gun at C.4.b.3.9 was laid and when transport came to a standstill fire was opened and transport was heard to move in an opposite direction immediately at an unexpected speed. BOVIS TRENCH was kept under observation by forward sections but no enemy movement was noticed. Some movement noticed in COPSE TRENCH and in sunken road at V.15.a.7.9 intermittent shelling from the direction of QUEANT in groups of 8 (6.7) mm and 2.5.9	True
	13		Enemy aircraft again engaged from C.5.a.1.t. about 200 rounds fired. At 8.30 pm transport again heard at U.24.a.1.9 and fire was at once opened from C.4.b.3.9. The enemy opened at once and two MG's hit shots very high. Shot made to suggest that the work cannot out by one M.G. and the 12th unit was no effective.	True
	14		Early quiet day. Intermittent shelling. PTE HEADINGTON wounded by shrapnel 7.30 am. 500 rounds fired at enemy aircraft. Movement observed from C.5.a.3.3 about 250 wounded fired at intervals between dusk and dawn. At about 9.30 pm a large party observed passing point U.12.c.5.2 going in the direction of HENDECOURT and party consisted of a wagon followed by about 30 men in file. L/Cpl. SHOTTER seriously wounded carrying to dug out entrance before blown in at 1 PM.	True

Army Form C. 2118.

WAR DIARY
or
INTELLIGENCE SUMMARY.
(Erase heading not required.)

Instructions regarding War Diaries and Intelligence Summaries are contained in F. S. Regs., Part II. and the Staff Manual respectively. Title pages will be prepared in manuscript.

Place	Date	Hour	Summary of Events and Information	Remarks and references to Appendices
In the line	1917 July 15		Quiet day. The company were relieved by 201 MG Coy, newly composite 4 am. Company proceeded to camp near MORY.	Fine
MORY	16		No parade. Till 6 PM the limbers proposed owing to warning order to move at 3 hours notice were cancelled at 12 midnight. Inspection of Iron Rations. Gun appliances to testing & repairing known	Fine Fine
	17		Physical Drill. Testing guns & gun equipment	Fine
	18		Physical Training. Company Drill. Drill of Elementary Training Mechanism	Fine
	19		3.30 Company parade. Physical Training. Mechanism. Immediate action, Section or Co-operation	Fine Fine
	20		Physical Training. Stoppages. Drill of Elementary Training M.G. Signals and Cleaning Guns	Fine
	21		Physical Training. Mechanism. Stoppages. Lecture by Section Officers	Fine
	22		Physical Training. Company Drill. Cleaning	Fine
	23		No. 1 & 3 Section 15 members. In Company Hrs 1 & 3 section moved into camp at LOGEAST WOOD G.2 & 3.6.	Fine
	24		Physical Training. Gun Drill. Immediate Action. Checking & cleaning of spare parts.	Rain Drill
LOGEAST WOOD	25			

WAR DIARY or INTELLIGENCE SUMMARY

Army Form C. 2118.

Place	Date	Hour	Summary of Events and Information	Remarks and references to Appendices
LOC EAST WOOD	1917 Jan 26		Physical Training. Stoppages of Elementary Training. Arms Drill. M.G. Sipson Lecture. Drill.	
	27		No 1.3 Section returned by 5 Corps Cavalry. Physical Training. Gun Drill. Arms Drill. Drill.	
	28		Physical Training. Arms Drill. Immediate Action. Commanders when proceed to England on leave.	Snow Wet
	29		Physical Training. Gun Drill. Company Drill.	
	30		Physical Training. Contours from Drill. Lecture by Lieut. Shen on Field Engineering. Lt. C.S. FELTON proceeded to M.G. School CAMIERS	Changeable

215 MACHINE GUN COMPANY.

O.C.

L OC EAST WOOD

WAR DIARY
or
INTELLIGENCE SUMMARY.
(Erase heading not required.)

Army Form C. 2118.

Place	Date July	Hour	Summary of Events and Information	Remarks and references to Appendices
LOG EAST WOOD	1"		Church Parade	
	2"		Physical Drill Gun Drill Stripping Guns and cleaning	
	3"		Physical Drill Inspection Guns Appliances from various Sections	
	4"		G.O.C's Inspection. Baths.	
	5"	2 P.M.	Company left camp at LOG EAST WOOD and marched to BANCOURT arriving 6.15 p.m. and encamping for the night.	
	6"	2 A.M.	Left camp at BANCOURT and marched to YTRES arriving 5 p.m. Huts were occupied for night.	
	7"		Sections left YTRES marches to HAVRINCOURT WOOD prior to proceeding to the line. Transport remained at YTRES. (Met.)	
	8"		Relief 126 & 127 M.G.Coys. Relief completed at 2.30 a.m.	
			10 Guns took up position in front line. 2 Guns in subsidiary line and 4 in reserve line. Guns carried out raids fire and engaged targets at K.27 d. 30. C.K.27 d.59. Enemy retaliates with Gasshells and M.G. fire.	57c NE. 57c SW.
	9"		Gun at K 2 c. 77 engaged targets in HAVRINCOURT WOOD and Village fired about 1000 rounds.	
	10		M.G.'s again fired on HAVRINCOURT VILLAGE and right end of	

Army Form C. 2118.

WAR DIARY or INTELLIGENCE SUMMARY.
(Erase heading not required.)

Place	Date	Hour	Summary of Events and Information	Remarks and references to Appendices
9th Corps	July			
	10th		HAVRINCOURT PARK. Targets engaged at K.27.a.4.3. and K.27.c.6.7. K.28.c.25. and fired about 2000 rounds. Enemy retaliated ALFRED ROAD and MONTMARRE. Enemy quiet for remainder of day. Pte Roper wounded.	Obsy.
	11th		Quiet day own m.g.'s engaged targets at K.37.c.0.9 WIGAN COPSE K.32.c.50.60 rounds fired 3000. Pte Warren and WHITFIELD wounded.	Obsy.
	12th		Enemy Aeroplanes more active. No 3 team No 2 sec relieves No 4 team No 2 section.	Obsy.
	13th		1 Draught Horse sent to Mobile Vetinary Sec. Gun fired on targets at K.32.a.45.45. NEW TRENCH. 1000 rounds fired. No7 team moved to Q.d.40.80. Tunnel emplacement commenced at Junction of trench and B. Reys. Targets engaged at K.33.c. K.27.c.	Obsy.
	14th		Intermittent enemy shelling m.g. engaged targets at K.33.c.10.20 K.32.a. + K.26.6. rounds fired about 1500.	Obsy.
	15th		Very quiet m.g.'s fired at HAVRINCOURT WOOD and PARK. WIGAN COPSE. about 2000 rounds fired. Enemy Aeroplanes fairly active.	Obsy.

Army Form C. 2118.

WAR DIARY
or
INTELLIGENCE SUMMARY.
(Erase heading not required.)

Instructions regarding War Diaries and Intelligence Summaries are contained in F. S. Regs., Part II. and the Staff Manual respectively. Title pages will be prepared in manuscript.

Place	Date	Hour	Summary of Events and Information	Remarks and references to Appendices
	July 16		No 9 Gun withdrawn to CHQ. owing to damaged MG. taking over position. MG's engaged targets at K28.c.25 K34.a.9.6. K33.6. rounds fired 1500	OBF.
	17		One team Number 3 Section with drawn from intermediate line and placed in YORKSHIRE BANK K 32.a. 5.8. to cover night bombing attack and lift of Battalion front. 1 team & No 3 Sec. withdrawn from intermediate line and brought to C.H.Q. 60737 Driver Fowler Killed 11 pm. Two guns engaged targets at K 28. c 2.5 and K 34 a. 9.6 rounds fired 4.500. Engels were also engaged at VESUVIUS. HAVRINCOURT WOOD and PARK rounds fired 4.500 (Mk)	OBF.
	18		Lieut HODGSON wounded (concussion) 57013 Pte Laurence. Killed. 17754 Pte Ruffle. Died of wounds. Targets engaged at K 32 c. r K 32 a. rounds fired 1500 (Vine)	OBF.
	19		Owing to casualties is was necessary to move gun at K 32 b.6 to K 32 a. 9.7 Fire was opened on K 33. c. K 27 a. 30.00 and K 27. b.5.0 and 1500 rounds were fired Immediately after the first burst A Horn (apparently used for calling statitions stations nearer) was sounded in enemy front positions and an enemy m.g. fired over own gun position from a bearing of 145°. At 11PM 1 Section of 198 M.S.Co relieved No 4 Section which retired to manoeuvre at S.HUBERTS CROSS.	OBF.
	20		No 1 Section and 1 team of No 3 relieved No 2 Section and one team of No 3 Section in left sector Enemy shelled front and support lines during day and at 10.30 pm put down an intense barrage followed by 15 minute box barrage. At 10.36 the enemy raided in a force estimated 120 men 2 officers. Immediate S.O.S. signal was put up two guns firing in direct laying line and these fired in conjunction with two guns at YORKSHIRE BANK 1500 rounds under plight line. Enemy raid was unsuccessful.	OBF.

WAR DIARY
or
INTELLIGENCE SUMMARY.
(Erase heading not required.)

Army Form C. 2118.

Place	Date JULY	Hour	Summary of Events and Information	Remarks and references to Appendices
	20.	11.15 PM	On account of casualties sustained by night Gun team of left sector and to ascertain whether observation was being obtained by the enemy on the Gun position 2/Lt ARNOLD and Sgt. WILFORD set out to reconnoitre enemy mine dugout at YORKSHIRE BANK in K.3.b. Crawling up to the dug out it was noticed that a pit in rear contained ammunition apparently used for German light machine Gun and a Eventually flash bombs. Voices were heard in the dug out and upon a Mills grenade being thrown in German rifles and escapes under a sharp rifle fire from our infantry. The Patrol returned safely.	AYJ
	21.		Quiet day, intermittent shelling. Targets engaged at K.3.d + K.27.c. rounds fired 700.	AYJ
	22.		Quiet day. at t. 10.30 p.m. raiding party (2 Off 60 OR) entered enemy position at CHALK PIT and captures 2 prisoners and much weapons informat. M.G.'s assisted raid by bringing fire to bear on HAVRINCOURT PK + WOOD, + MON COP.	AYJ
	23.		Very Quiet day; at 11.15 p.m. (1 Off. 30 OR) raided enemy position WIGAN COPSE in K.26.d. assisted by M.G. Barrage. Result. 5 enemy killed and wounded. No retaliation by enemy;	AYJ
	24.		Very Quiet. no machine fire owing to patrol being out. (Fine)	AYJ

WAR DIARY or INTELLIGENCE SUMMARY.

(Erase heading not required.)

Army Form C. 2118.

Place	Date	Hour	Summary of Events and Information	Remarks and references to Appendices
	25.		Intermittent shelling of OXFORD VALLEY and YORKSHIRE BANK. A Raiding Party 2/o 1 Offr and 20 O.R. with 2 Lewis Guns raided piquet at K.33.d.85.10 with assistance of Artillery m.g's & Trench mortars but without result. Targets engaged throughout the 24 hours, MOW COPSE, BOGGARTS HOLE. No Retaliation. (Fine)	Copy 1 Offr Copy Copy Copy
	26.		Enemy very quiet and M.G's did not fire.	Copy
	27. 28.		Company relieved by 26 M.Co. relief completed by 11.30 p.m. Company marches back to Billets at YTRES. (Fine)	Copy
	29.		Company paraded at 6.30 a.m. and proceeded by Bus and Train to SAULTY. and from there marched into billets at BERNEVILLE.	Copy
	30.	3.45 a.m.	Company arrives BERNEVILLE, and rested during day.	Copy
	31.		Kit Inspections, clothing renewed. Rifles cleaned and reports. Company Paid.	Copy

O.B. Kellar Lieut
215 M.G. Co.

To 58th Divisional Headquarters

From O.C. 215 M.G. Company.

I enclose herewith War Diary of this Unit for the month of August 1917, please

[Signature] O.C.
215 Machine Gun Company.

Army Form C. 2118.

WAR DIARY
or
INTELLIGENCE SUMMARY.
(Erase heading not required.)

Instructions regarding War Diaries and Intelligence Summaries are contained in F.S. Regs., Part II. and the Staff Manual respectively. Title pages will be prepared in manuscript.

215 COMPANY MACHINE GUN CORPS

Place	Date AUG	Hour	Summary of Events and Information	Remarks and references to Appendices
BERNEVILLE	1	9.6.1.	Physical Drill. Ammo Drill. Saluting Drill. Combined Drill.	C.J.F.
-do-	2.	9.6.1.	Interior Economy. N°4 Section less one section proceeded to ANZIN & LOUEZ on Anti Aircraft Duty.	C.J.F.
-do-	3.	9.6.1.	Physical Training. Section Inspection. Immediate Action. Combined Drill and Close order Drill.	C.J.F.
-do-	4	9.6.1.	Physical Training. C.O's Inspection. Winter Pack mule Drill.	C.J.F.
do.	5.		Church Parades.	C.J.F.
do.	6	9.6.1.	Sections under Section Officers & Close order Drill.	C.J.F.
-do.	7.	9.6.1.	Company tactics: Stoppages practice fired on Range.	C.J.F.
-do.	8.	8.30/6 pm.	Brigade practice attack scheme; Pay of Company.	C.J.F. C.J.F.
-do.	9	9.6.1.	Physical Training. Inspection Limber Gun Drill with Gas Helmets ammo drill and map work:	C.J.F.
-do.	10	9.6.6.	Brigade General- Athletic and sports. DAINVILLE.	C.J.F.
-do.	11.		Interior economy;	C.J.F.

Army Form C. 2118.

WAR DIARY
or
INTELLIGENCE SUMMARY.
(Erase heading not required.)

Instructions regarding War Diaries and Intelligence Summaries are contained in F. S. Regs., Part II. and the Staff Manual respectively. Title pages will be prepared in manuscript.

215 COMPANY MACHINE GUN CORPS

Place	Date	Hour	Summary of Events and Information	Remarks and references to Appendices
BERNEVILLE	Aug 12.		Church Parade.	
	13.	9/1	Physical Training Inspection tobac order Drill Combined Drill Immediate action	
	14.	9.51	Physical Training Inspection by C.O. Kindes stack mule drill	
	15.	9.4.M.	Brigade scheme.	
	16.	9.51.	Physical Training Section Officers Gas Drill Use of Clinometer Map work. Pay of Company	
	17.	9.51.	Route March	
	18.	9.51.	Physical Training Inspectors Iron Rators Gas appliances Kit etc.	
	19		School Parades.	
	20.		Games Baths Physical Training Gas Drill Cleaning and repairing Limbers.	

WAR DIARY
or
INTELLIGENCE SUMMARY.
(Erase heading not required.)

Army Form C. 2118.

Place	Date	Hour	Summary of Events and Information	Remarks and references to Appendices
BERNEVILLE	Aug 9: 21	7AM & 4 PM.	Divisional Scheme.	99f.
	22		Physical Training; Section Officers inspection of Gas appliances limber and pack mule drill	93f.
	23		Physical Training company drill lecture by Section Officers	93f.
	24		Company left BERNEVILLE. Transport left at 1 am remainder of company at 2.15 am and marched to ARRAS station	93f.
	"	7AM	Company entrained at ARRAS.	
		4:30 PM.	do. detrained at PROVEN and marched to BRAKE camp. St JOHNS WOOD, arrived about 9 PM.	
	25		Cleaning Guns and limber. Inspection Gas appliances	93f.
	26		Gas Helmet Drill Church Parade;	93f.
	27		Inspection of Ammunition talk packing Guns in limbers	93f.

WAR DIARY
or
INTELLIGENCE SUMMARY
(Erase heading not required.)

Army Form C. 2118.

Place	Date	Hour	Summary of Events and Information	Remarks and references to Appendices
	Aug. 28.		The Company less transport left BRAKE Camp at 7.30 p.m. and marched to REIGERSBERG Camp.	P.J.
	29/30.		No 3 & 4 sections relieved 2 sections 206 M.G.Coy. No 4 section took over position in front line 2 guns at SPRING FIELD and 2 guns at JANET FARM. No 3 section took over position in support line near CHEDDAR VILLA. No 1 & 2 section remained in reserve at RIEGERSBERG Camp. Transport lines moved to POTTEN FARM from BRAKE LINES CAMP.	P.J.
	31.		Day very quiet indiscriminate shelling. Enemy M.G.'s not firing.	P.J.

O.B. Gibbs Major
O/C 215 M.G. Co.

27

To Headquarters
 56th Division

From O.C 175th Infantry Brigade

I enclose herewith amended War Diary for the month of September 1917.
please

"A"
Passed to you
L. Moulton
Capt

O.C
215 Machine Gun Company.

WAR DIARY or INTELLIGENCE SUMMARY

Army Form C. 2118.

215 M.G. Coy

Place	Date	Hour	Summary of Events and Information	Remarks and references to Appendices
LINE	1/9/17		In the line. Quiet in front line. Indirect fire from reserve guns in CANOPUS TRENCH on to trenches east of WINNIPEG.	M.D.D.
-"-	2/9/17		Nos. 1 & 2 Sections relieved 3 & 4 Sections on the line. No. 2 Section in front line, and No. 1 Section in reserve in CANOPUS TRENCH. During the night reserve section fired on TIRPITZ FARM. 1500 rounds being expended. During the evening from SPRINGFIELD (map ref. C.12.b.3.6) a party of about 100 enemy were seen moving across the skyline towards WINNIPEG, about 300x distant and were promptly dealt with by our machine guns and rifle fire. Casualties and men promises afterwards taken. They suffered heavy casualties. Fine weather. Brilliant moon at night. Intermittent shelling during the day. 2 guns at SPRINGFIELD escorted minor operation of the infantry who established a post at SPOT FARM. The guns were placed with a view to covering the left flank. The post was established without opposition. These guns did not fire.	M.D.D. sheet POELCAPPELLE 1/9/17
-"-	3/9/17		Support guns carried out indirect fire throughout the night on trenches behind WINNIPEG. 2000 rounds expended. SPOT FARM was reconnoitred with a view to placing a gun there. On approaching SPOT FARM [struck through: reconnoitring party was challenged by a German post near the CEMETERY...]	M.D.D.
-"-	4/9/17		The reconnoitring party was challenged by a German post near the CEMETERY. Owing to the comparatively ample field of fire, and to the cover afforded by the road to enemy patrol which might come from the CEMETERY it was considered inadvisable to place a gun in that position.	M.D.D.
-"-	5/9/17		Between 9.20 p.m - 9.45 p.h. and 10 p.m - 10.30 p.m gun at SPRINGFIELD fired on enemy movement east of SPOT FARM covered by our steady artillery barrage; 2000 rounds expended. Indirect fire carried out from CANOPUS TRENCH on area about A.7.c.3.4 and A.7.a.2.2. 2 Officers and 32 O.R. proceeded to HOUTKERQUE on Battle Supplies but were recalled immediately to Coy H.Q.	M.D.D. sheet POELCAPPELLE 5/9/17

WAR DIARY
or
INTELLIGENCE SUMMARY.
(Erase heading not required.)

Army Form C. 2118.

215 COMPANY MACHINE GUN CORPS

Instructions regarding War Diaries and Intelligence Summaries are contained in F. S. Regs., Part II. and the Staff Manual respectively. Title pages will be prepared in manuscript.

Place	Date	Hour	Summary of Events and Information	Remarks and references to Appendices
LINE	6/9/17		Nos 3 & 4 Sections relieved Nos 1 & 2 Sections. No 3 Section in front line and No 4 Section in support. In response to S.O.S. signal the guns at JANET FARM fired 1000 rounds in attack maintenance	A.D.D.
-"-	7/9/17		Reserve guns in CANIPUS TRENCH fired 1300 rounds on tracks east of WINNIPEG	A.D.D. POELCAPPELLE 1/10,000 A.D.D.
-"-	8/9/17	2.30 p.m	Gas was released against the CEMETERY MEBUS (map ref C.12.d.4.9). 5 guns in the front line + 3 guns in reserve co-operated with the infantry in minor operation which was carried out with a view to capturing WINNIPEG - JURY FARM and the CEMETERY. Zero hour 9.45 p.m. 3 guns at JANET FARM fired from 8.30 p.m to 9.30 p.m on to JURY FARM, WINNIPEG and the CEMETERY with a view to preventing enemy front troops being brought up before Zero hour. 4000 rounds were fired. At 9.30 p.m 2 guns advanced to "A" post (map Ref C.12.d.6.7) for the purpose of covering the right flank in case of counter-attack. 2 guns at SPRINGFIELD fired 1000 rounds between Zero and Zero + 10 minutes on ground east of SPOT FARM in order to cover the advance of the infantry from SPRINGFIELD to the CEMETERY.	A.D.D.
-"-	9/9/17	3.0 a.m	Owing to the withdrawal of the infantry from JURY FARM the 2 guns at "A" post withdrew to their original positions at JANET FARM.	A.D.D.
-"-	10/9/17		Harassing fire was carried out from reserve guns. 2000 rounds were fired. Nothing else of importance occurred.	A.D.D.
-"-	11/9/17	3.0 a.m to 5.0 a.m	The enemy shelled all area between ST JULIEN and 1000 x east of YPRES CANAL with gas shell. The Company was relieved in the line by 206 M.G. Company: strength of previous relief 1000 rounds were fired by the reserve guns on usual tracks.	A.D.D.

WAR DIARY
or
INTELLIGENCE SUMMARY.
(Erase heading not required.)

Army Form C. 2118.

Place	Date	Hour	Summary of Events and Information	Remarks and references to Appendices
LINE	12/9/17	1.30 a.m	Relief complete. Sections proceeded to REIGERSBERG CAMP.	A.D.D.
REIGERSBERG CAMP	12/9/17	4.0 p.m	Company marches to BRAKE CAMP. Transport lines remaining at POTTEN FARM.	A.D.D.
BRAKE CAMP	13/9/17		Inspection of Gas Helmets. Inauguration of and inspection of guns & personnel. Company paid.	A.D.D.
-"-	14/9/17		A party of 24 men from the 2/9"., 2/10"., 2/11"., and 2/12"., Batt: London Regt. reported to the Company as attached men. Physical Drill. Lecturing limbers and preparing same.	A.D.D.
-"-	15/9/17		Physical Drill. Section Officers inspection. Technical instruction of attached men. Church Parade.	A.D.D.
-"-	16/9/17		Arms Drill. Section Officers inspection. Gun Drill. Camp cleaning. 15 O.R. of 175". L.T.M.B. attached to Coy. 14 O.R. of 2/9". Bn. London Regt. returned to their Units. Making "Tommy" Cookers.	A.D.D.
-"-	17/9/17			A.D.D.
-"-	18/9/17	9.30 a.m 10.30-12.30 p.m	C.O's inspection. Learning Drill & bath.	A.D.D. Sheet POELCAPPELLE 110570
		6.30 p.m	Company was conveyed to CANAL BANK in motor lorries, and from they proceeded by track to the BUND (map ref C.11.c.9.8) No 3 Section relieved the section 214 M.G. Coy at MON DU HIBOU (map ref C.6.c.2.4.) No 4 Section relieved 2 guns at REGINA CROSS, and 2 guns in THE BUND, also 214 M.G. Coy. Nos. 1 & 2 Sections remained in dug-outs in the BUND.	

Army Form C. 2118.

WAR DIARY
or
INTELLIGENCE SUMMARY.
(Erase heading not required.)

Place	Date	Hour	Summary of Events and Information	Remarks and references to Appendices
LINE	19.9.17	9.0 p.m	No. 3 Section relieved by a section of 98 M.G Company at MON DU HIBOU, and withdrawn to THE BUND. No 4 Section withdrawn from their positions without being relieved. All the Sections in THE BUND made preparations for barrage fire. Company H.Q. were established at THE BUND.	M.D.D
-"-	20.9.17	5.45 a.m	174 + 173 Infantry Brigades attacked as shewn on attached map. Barrage fire was carried out from THE BUND by all 16 guns with times + targets as shewn on attached map. 140,000 rounds were fired, no gun overheated or prolonged stoppage. 2 men were slightly wounded. The infantry reported favourably on the shooting. When the barrage fire was finished, the guns were dismounted and the section remained in THE BUND	H.D.D
-"-	21.9.17		175th Infantry Brigade relieved 173rd + 174th Brigades on the line. Machine guns were placed as follows:- (A) front line guns. 4 guns at CUSTER HOUSES and WURST FARM 2 -"- -"- VON TIRPITZ FARM 2 -"- -"- STROPPE FARM (B) support guns 2 guns at SPRINGFIELD 2 -"- -"- "A" post	H.D.D
-"-	22.9.17	4.0 a.m	Relief complete. 2 guns at WURST FARM fired 1000 rounds on enemy assembling at KRONPRINTZ FARM; the body of men was broken up.	H.D.D
-"-	23.9.17	6.30 a.m 7.00 p.m	Lieut Annett captured 3 prisoners in front of STROPPE FARM. At 7.30 p.m the enemy counter attacked between STROPPE FARM and GUESSE FARM. The 2 guns at STROPPE FARM assembled in driving the enemy off. Lieut J.C. Plummer was killed near "A" post.	H.D.D

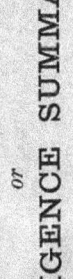

215 COMPANY MACHINE GUN CORPS

WAR DIARY or INTELLIGENCE SUMMARY

Army Form C. 2118.

(Erase heading not required.)

Place	Date	Hour	Summary of Events and Information	Remarks and references to Appendices
LINE	24/9/17	11 a.m.	Small party of enemy attempted to enter OLIVE HOUSE. 1 gun at CLUSTER HOUSES fired at the party, which was driven off with casualties.	A.D.D.
"	25/9/17		Nos 1 & 2 Sections were relieved in the line as follows:— No 3 Section and No 2 sub section of No 4 Section assembled at CLUSTER HOUSES. No 2 sub section of No 1 Section remained in position at WURST FARM. The 2 guns at VON TIRPITZ FARM were relieved by No 1 sub section of No 4 Section. The 2 guns at STROPPE FARM were relieved by 2 guns of 198 M.G. Company (temporarily attached to 215 M.G. Company)	A.D.D.
"	26/9/17	4 a.m.	Relief complete. No 2 Section to CANOPUS TRENCH.	A.D.D.
		5.50 a.m.	The 2/9 & 2/12 Battns, London Regt. attacked the BLUE LINE on eleven an attached map. At the time of the attack it was still fairly dark whilst a very heavy mist made impossible to see more than a few yards off. About 6 a.m. No 3 Section and the 2 guns of No 4 Section moved forward from CLUSTER HOUSES to WURST FARM. The 2 guns of No 1 Section remained in position at WURST FARM. Owing to the thick mist all the gun teams completely lost touch with the Infantry. In a result of this, 2/Lieuts. HOWLETT & YOUNG went forward to reconnoitre and to endeavour to find out the situation. They ascertained that the 2/12 & Battn. had captured CAIRO, but had not taken SVAKIM. 2/Lieut. HOWLETT at once ordered Sgt. ROWNEY to take up with the 2 guns teams of No 4 Section about 200x West of SVAKIM. 2/Lieut. YOUNG then led No 3 Section	ACTION OF GUNS AT CLUSTER HOUSES UNDER THE COMMAND OF 2/LIEUT. HOWLETT.

WAR DIARY
or
INTELLIGENCE SUMMARY.

Army Form C. 2118.

215 COMPANY MACHINE GUN CORPS

Place	Date	Hour	Summary of Events and Information	Remarks and references to Appendices
LINE	26/9/17	8.0 a.m	forward in the direction of DEAR HOUSE, and eventually got into action at DEAR HOUSE. A report was received from 2/Lieut HOWLETT stating that No 3 Section was in action at DEAR HOUSE and that he was then going forward to ascertain if the Infantry had yet captured BOETLEER. This he did and whilst doing so was killed, almost at the same time 2/Lieut YOUNG was severely wounded and Sgt BROTHERHOOD killed showing the fire of their gun against the enemy at SVAKIM. Lee Cpl STREET was now in charge of the Section. As the infantry had failed to capture BOETLEER the whole of No 3 Section remained in action at DEAR HOUSE for the rest of the day. During the day the gun fired frequently at parties of the enemy seen moving in different localities and heavy casualties were inflicted.	HDD
		6 p.m	The enemy put down a heavy barrage on our front and on the SUNKEN on the night. Soon after this the Sunken on our right was seen to be retiring and a little later our own infantry began to relieve No 3 Section hung on to their position until after the infantry on either side of them had retired, and they themselves retired to a position about 100x east of OLIVE HOUSE which was then the front line. At the same time the 2 gun team under Sgt DOWNEY withdrew to CAIRO during the retirement Lee Cpl STREET was killed leaving Lee Cpl RICE in charge of the Section. On learning of No 3 Section's casualties, Sgt DOWNEY left Lee Cpl RICE in No 2 gun and took charge of No 3 Section and established them in their new	

Army Form C. 2118.

WAR DIARY
or
INTELLIGENCE SUMMARY.
(Erase heading not required.)

Instructions regarding War Diaries and Intelligence Summaries are contained in F.S. Regs., Part II. and the Staff Manual respectively. Title pages will be prepared in manuscript.

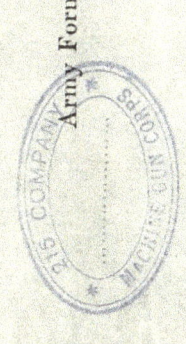

Place	Date	Hour	Summary of Events and Information	Remarks and references to Appendices
LINE	20/9/17		position. During the retirement one gun of No 3 Section was lost owing to casualties. So the position at about 7 am was:- 3 guns No 3 Section near OLIVE HOUSE 2 --- No 4 --- at CAIRO During the bombardment no hostile counter attack was observed.	H.D.D.
		6 am	These two guns moved forward in the direction of VALE HOUSE. As the Infantry, who were to have captured WINZIG, had suffered heavy casualties, and had failed to do so, 2/Lieut HEAP ordered his guns to dig in at VALE HOUSE, which he had reached in spite of heavy M.G. fire by crawling forward. Whilst getting forward to this position 2/Lieut HEAP was severely wounded, Sgt PEARCE killed, and about 4 other ranks hit	ACTION OF 2 GUNS UNDER 2/LIEUT HEAP.
		6 pm	The Infantry that was left also retired, and these 2 guns had to be brought back to nearly their original position, about 100 x east of VON TIRPITZ FARM, where they remained until relief.	ACTION OF RESERVE GUNS
		2.30 pm	The enemy began to shell our lines steadily, the OCs 2/9th & 2/12th Battn London Regts asked for reinforcements to be sent up, as a result No 2 Section were ordered to move to CLUSTER HOUSES with the reserve battalion (3/10th Bn London Regt). Lieut ARNOLD got his	
		3.30 pm	guns into action between WURST FARM and CLIFTON HOUSE, and fired on about 200 of the	

WAR DIARY
or
INTELLIGENCE SUMMARY.
(Erase heading not required.)

Army Form C. 2118.

Place	Date	Hour	Summary of Events and Information	Remarks and references to Appendices
LINE	26/9/17		Enemy who went over were moving forward towards KRONPRINZ FARM, but there was no hostile movement on our Brigade front except by ones and twos who went mostly running away afterwards. ARNOLD pieced 2 of his guns with a platoon of the 2/4th sth London Regt. about 250x east of CLIFTON HOUSE but at 6 p.m. this platoon also returned.	H.D.D.
LINE	27/9/17	6 p.m.	Enemy again put down a very heavy barrage along a whole front, and the S.O.S. was sent up on both sides of the Brigade. No infantry counter-attack materialised and the situation became quiet about 8 p.m. 2 guns near VON TIRPITZ FARM were relieved during the night by 2 guns of 143 M.G. Company, whilst 4 guns of 177 M.G. Company relieved 4 of our guns at OLIVE HOUSE & CLUSTER HOUSES. Remaining guns were withdrawn.	H.D.D.
REIGERSBERG CAMP	28/9/17	5 a.m. 4.30 p.m.	Relief completed. Section moved to REIGERSBERG CAMP on completion of relief. Company marched to RAMBRE CAMP.	H.D.D.
RAMBRE CAMP	29/9/17		Company rested and no parades were ordered.	H.D.D.
-"-	30/9/17	11.30 a.m. 6.30 a.m.	Company marched to BRAKE CAMP, preparatory to move on 1st Oct. by train to BERTHAM. A portion of the Transport proceeded by road march to BERTHAM.	H.D.D.

H.D. Orek. Capt.
215 MACHINE GUN COMPANY.

To Headquarters
58th Division

From O.C. 215 M.G. Company.

I enclose herewith War Diary of this Unit for the month of October 1917. please

[signature] Lt. M.
O.C.
215 MACHINE GUN COMPANY.

WAR DIARY
or
INTELLIGENCE SUMMARY

Army Form C. 2118.

(Erase heading not required.)

215 M.G. Coy Vol 8

Place	Date	Hour	Summary of Events and Information	Remarks and references to Appendices
BRAKE CAMP	1/10/17		Camps cleaning and preparing for move on night 1 1/2 October	
		8.30pm	A party of 100 men marche off from BRAKE CAMP to PESELHOEK for the purpose of loading tactical train	Fine
		10.15pm	Remainder of Company marched to PESELHOEK for entrainment	
BERTHAM	2/10/17	1.45am	Company left PESELHOEK by train and arrived at AUDRICQUES at 8am. After unloading train the Company proceeded by route march to BERTHAM arriving 12.45pm where billets were occupied.	Fine
			Lieut. J. McKINLAY HILLCOAT joined Coy from Base Depot	
			— J.R. LAMBERTON	
			2/Lt. E & P ELFORY	1.10.17
			— G.E. LEE	
	3.10.17	9.30am	Inspection by C.O.	
		10.30 – 12 noon	Cleaning clothing boots & gun equipment	
	4.10.17	9 – 9.15 am	Section Officers Inspection	
		9.15 – 10.0	Company Lewis	
		10.0 – 12.15pm	Billets filling, Kit inspection, cleaning lorries	
		12.15 – 1.0	Rifle oil and bandrs	
			Pay out of Company	
			33 O.R. from 3/10 Batt absorbed for instruction 14 O.R. joined from Base	Fine
			Baths allotted, citadel at REEQUES	
	5.10.17	8am – 12 Noon	Close order drill for No 4 Section extended men Closer order drill for No 1 + 2 Sections	
		9 – 9.15 am		
		9 – 12 Noon		
		2.0 – 3.0pm	Barrage drill	
			Bayonet Combat established in Coys camp billeting area	Fine

WAR DIARY
or
INTELLIGENCE SUMMARY.

(Erase heading not required.)

Army Form C. 2118.

Place	Date	Hour	Summary of Events and Information	Remarks and references to Appendices
BERTHAM	6.10.17	9-9.15 AM	Section Officers Inspection	
		9.15-10.0	Gas order drill	
		10.0-11.0	Rapid stoppages, assembling and annual gun drill	
		11.15-12.15 AM		Fine
	7.10.17	8 AM	1 officer & 20 o.r. proceeded by motor lorry to CALAIS for a day's trip	
		10.30 AM	Inspection of billets by C.O.	
		11.0 AM	Church parade to C of E owing to inclemency of weather cancelled	Wet
	8.10.17	AM	Section Officers Inspection	
		9.0-9.15	Company Drill	
		9.15-10.0	T.O.E.T	
		10.15-11 PM	Barrage Drill	
		11.30-12.30	Immediate action & stoppages drill without bar respirators	Wet
		2.0-3.0 PM		
	9.10.17	9-9.15 AM	Section Officers Inspection	
		9.15-10.0	Company drill	
		10.15-11.15	T.O.E.T	
		11.30-12.30	Immediate action & stoppages with and without bar respirator	
		2.0-3.0	Barrage Drill	Fine
	10.10.17	9-9.15 AM	Section officers Inspection	
		9.15-10.0	Company drill	
		10.15-11.0	Swabbing out guns & gun equipment for inspection	
		11.0	Inspection of guns & gun equipment	
		2.0-3.0 PM	Barrage drill	
			9 men under Lt HELTON proceeded to REST CAMP 3 men S.P. BOULOGNE for 7 days	Fine

WAR DIARY or INTELLIGENCE SUMMARY

Army Form C. 2118.

Place	Date	Hour	Summary of Events and Information	Remarks and references to Appendices
BERTHAM	11.10.17	AM 9.0-9.30	Physical Training	
		9.45-10.0	Section Officers Inspection	
		10.0-12.30	Stripping locks, mopping out, practice ammunition	
		pm 2.0-3.30	Preparing guns for range	
	12.10.17	7.30am	Company proceeds to 'B' range S.J NORDAUSQUES	wet
	13.10.17		Ranks received from 9.0-12.0 AM Proceeds to RECQUES	wet
		9.0-12.0	Section Officers inspection of canvas tent, gas apparatus &	
		10.30	YOKON Pack completion under Coy orderly Sergt	wet
			PACK PONY inspection by G.O.C - cancelled owing to weather	
	14.10.17	AM 10.15	Church parade to C.O.E and 2/Lt Bass at NIELLES	fine
		11.0	G.O.C's Conference - Co 2nd command and T.O. present	fine
	15.10.17	9 am	Company parades for Bde tactical scheme at NORDAUSQUES	
	16.10.17	9 AM	Section Officers Inspection	
		9.15-9.45	Bear-filling	
		9.45-12.30 pm	Care and Cleaning	
		2.0-3.30 am	Group on short range, I hour for section	
		4.0-4.30	Recommended of award of Military Medal to	fine
			58613 Sgt DONNEY J	
			63989 Pte SCHOFES E	
			announced award of Military Cross to	
			Lieut A.M. ARNOLD	

WAR DIARY
or
INTELLIGENCE SUMMARY.

(Erase heading not required.)

Army Form C. 2118.

Instructions regarding War Diaries and Intelligence Summaries are contained in F. S. Regs., Part II. and the Staff Manual respectively. Title pages will be prepared in manuscript.

Place	Date	Hour	Summary of Events and Information	Remarks and references to Appendices
BEAU HAM	17.10.17	8.45am	Company fall in all ready to march off 9.0 am for inspection and presentation of medal returned to recipients of recent awards	
			LIEUT. ANT. BRINDLY } SGT. DOWNEY }	
	18.10.17		Pay out of Company	
			No 1 Section parade 1.0 pm } to take part in practice attack with 2/10 & 11 12/13 Bn. respectively	
			2 — 8.30 am }	
			3 — 9.0 am }	
		am	No. 4 Section	
		9.0 9 pm	Section Officers Inspection	
		10.15 12.30	Rest fitting & practice firing on short range	
	19.10.17	9.0 am	Company & No 4 Section Section left to take part in Batt. +Bde. Practice attacks	
			Preparation of billets & orders for move to new area	
	20.10.17	4.9 am	Transport of packs less 5 GS Waggons and men cars and provenders hand coped to Rats Camp	
			Camp SC JAN TER BIEZEN with A.L.T. HT Convoy	
		9.30 am	Advance parts of I officer 3 OR 52 OR by lorry for new area	
		9.0 pm	Section Officers Inspection	
		10.15 10.30	Kit inspection	
		10.30 11.30	Under Section Officers	
	21.10.17	4.40 pm	Company less remainder of Transport proceeded by road march to AUDRICQUES STATION and entrained at 10 pm, detraining at HOPOUTRE proceeded by route march to ROAD CAMP S. JAN TER BIEZEN	
		9.45 pm	Remainder of Transport proceeded to AUDRICQUES STATION and entrained to HOPOUTRE	

Army Form C. 2118.

WAR DIARY
or
INTELLIGENCE SUMMARY.
(Erase heading not required.)

Instructions regarding War Diaries and Intelligence Summaries are contained in F. S. Regs., Part II. and the Staff Manual respectively. Title pages will be prepared in manuscript.

Place	Date	Hour	Summary of Events and Information	Remarks and references to Appendices
ROAD CAMP S'HERTOGENBOSCH	22.10.19	4.30 am	Company arrived at ROAD CAMP where felt tents & equipment were prepared. Transport parked about 1 mile distant from the Company	Fine
	23.10.19	9.10.0 am	No parade owing to wet weather	
		10.0-11.30	Refreshing trenches - Rest fining	
		2.0-5.0	Rest fining	
			Baths allowed Company	
	24.10.19	9.30 am	Company paraded & marched off to 15km post in a practice attack	Drive Drive Wet
		2.30 pm	Pay out of Company	
	25.10.19	9-12.30 am	Rest fining repairing railway trenches	
		2.0-5.30 pm	Gen Bowes inspects of Bns cooperation by Bn gm N.C.O	
		2.30-5.0	Rifle practice	Inst
	26.10.19	9.12.30 am	Repairing railway timbers for preselling up the line	
		2.0-5.30		Inst
			C.O. Maton Opinion presents by Rainche to recommittee the line	
	27.10.19	9.0-1.15	Inspection by Lieutn Officers	
		9.15-12.15	Instruction James Cat. 9pm. full to trainer of References	Wet
	28.10.19	11.0 am	Company parade for CPE	
		12.0 am	- Numbermanwell	
	29.10.19	8.30	Lecture Room Respite	
		9.15 am	Company Drill	
		10.12 am	Lectures out guns & ammunition for repairs	

WAR DIARY
or
INTELLIGENCE SUMMARY.
(Erase heading not required.)

Army Form C. 2118.

Instructions regarding War Diaries and Intelligence Summaries are contained in F. S. Regs., Part II. and the Staff Manual respectively. Title pages will be prepared in manuscript.

Place	Date	Hour	Summary of Events and Information	Remarks and references to Appendices
ROAD CAMP ELJANTER BIEZEN	29/10/17	11.p-12.n 2.0-4.0	Inspection of guns & equipment respecting limbers Reinspection & Inspection further works	Div
	30/10/17	6.0 am	No 3 M section & his Transport marched from ROAD CAMP to RAILHOEK PENTALUIZ with Army at KAIGERSBURG from where they proceeded to KEMPTON PARK being concentrated in huts and having themselves in readiness to relieve 197 M.G.Coy W for him on nights of 30/31 October	
		10.25 am	No 12 Section M.G. marched from ROAD CAMP to RAILHOEK and entrained subsequently OBREIEN from where they marched to SIEGE CAMP and were accommodated in huts. Arrived at Rlwy camp at 4.0 pm	
		8.0 am	Reptiling limbers of No 3 M section Coys out trident Coys proceeded by road to SIEGE CAMP arriving 11.30 am. Replying limbers & gun equipment of No 3 M section proceeded to KEMPTON PARK	
		10.0 am	Remnants of transport left ROAD CAMP and proceeded by road to SIEGE CAMP arriving 3.0 pm	
	31/10/17	3.0 pm 2.45 pm	No 3 M section entrained & section of 197 M.G.Coy in the time No 12 section proceeded to CANAL BANK Barrels, limbers & the 4 sections staying the transport remained out SIEGE CAMP	Ans Div

W. Hallam H.P.
O.C. 215 MACHINE GUN COMPANY.

QE 3·56'

GUN Nº	BATTERY Nº	BARRAGE	BEARING	DISTRIBUTION	
1	A	Nº 1	21° R	~~ELEVATION~~	
2	"	"	21° 40'R	4.0.	
3	"	"	22° 20'	4.0	
4	"	"	23°	4.0	
5	"	"	23° 40'	4.0	
6	"	"	24° 20'	4.0	
7	"	"	25°	4.0	RAPID
8	"	"	25° 40'	4.0	

GUN Nº	BATTERY Nº	BARRAGE	BEARING	DISTRIBUTION	
1	B.	Nº 1	26° 20	4.0.	
2	"	"	27°	4.0.	
3	"	"	27° 40	4.0.	
4	"	"	28° 20	4.0.	
5	"	"	29°	4.0.	RAPID
6	"	"	29° 40	4.0.	
7	"	"	30° 20	4.0.	
8	"	"	31°	4.0.	

QE 3°56' ZERO ZERO + 6

Q.E. 6°-11"

Gun Nº	Battery Nº	Barrage	Bearing	Distribution	Rate
1	A	Nº 2	30° R		
2	"	"	31°-10'	1°-10'	
3	"	"	32°-20'	1°-10'	
4	"	"	33°-30'	1°-10'	
5	"	"	34°-40'	1°-10'	
6	"	"	35°-50'	1°-10'	
7	"	"	37°	1°-10'	
8	"	"	38°-10'	1°-10'	

Gun Nº	Battery Nº	Barrage	Bearing	Distribution	Rate
1	B	Nº 2	37° R		
2	"	"	37°-35'	35'	
3	"	"	38°-10'	35'	
4	"	"	38°-45'	35'	
5	"	"	39°-20'	35'	
6	"	"	39°-55'	35'	
7	"	"	40°-30'	35'	
8	"	"	41°-5'	35'	

LEFT.   RIGHT.
4 GUNS 5°-30   4 GUNS. 6°-11"

ZERO+6 to ZERO + 1-33

Q E 7°-47'

Gun No	Battery No	Barrage	Bearing	Distribution	Rate
1	A	N°3	43° R	1°	
2	"	"	44°	1°	
3	"	"	45°	1°	
4	"	"	46°	1°	
5	"	"	47°	1°	
6	"	"	48°	1°	
7	"	"	49°	1°	
8	"	"	50°	1°	

ZERO+1-33 TO ZERO+2-33 CONTINUOUS.

Gun No	Battery	Barrage	Bearing	Distribution
1	B	N°3	46°	
2	"	"	47°	1°
3	"	"	48°	1°
4	"	"	49°	1°
5	"	"	50°	1°
6	"	"	51°	1°
7	"	"	52°	1°
8	"	"	53°	1°

LEFT 4 GUNS 6°-0'   RIGHT 4 GUNS 6°-31'

58th Division   14

From O.C. 215 M.G. Company

I enclose herewith Original War Diary for the month of November 1917, please.

.... O.C.
215 MACHINE GUN COMPANY.

WAR DIARY
or
INTELLIGENCE SUMMARY.
(Erase heading not required.)

Army Form C. 2118.

Place	Date	Hour	Summary of Events and Information	Remarks and references to Appendices
	NOV			
	1		Number 1+2 sections proceeded from Canal Bank to KEMPTON PARK. The positions of the gun how in the line were:- (1) 3 guns TRACAS (2) 2 guns MEUKER. (3) 2 guns HELLES (4) 1 gun at Y.14.a.2.2.	Ref Map SPRIET 1/40000. Off.
	2		Number 3 section relieved number 3+4 in the line. Guns of number 2 section were mounted in way sie. Guns are also as follows (1) Two TRACAS. (2) 1 at BREWERY but otherwise the same.	Off.
	3		Nothing of importance occurred.	Off.
	4		Water and Ration was sent up to the two sections in the line. Two of the carrying party were wounded: already both shelling on the Duckboard during the day.	Off.
	5		Fairly quiet day nothing to report.	Off.
	6		No 3+4 sections relieved numbers 1+2 in the line. One of the two guns at HELLES mounted to NOBLES FARM.	Off.

Army Form C. 2118.

WAR DIARY
or
INTELLIGENCE SUMMARY.
(Erase heading not required.)

Instructions regarding War Diaries and Intelligence Summaries are contained in F. S. Regs., Part II. and the Staff Manual respectively. Title pages will be prepared in manuscript.

Place	Date Nov	Hour	Summary of Events and Information	Remarks and references to Appendices
	7.	2 P.M.	A practice Barrage manifested by our own Artillery. There was some short shooting near GLOUCESTER FARM. Nothing else to report.	
	8.		Numbers 1 & 2 sections left KEMPTON PARK in Busses and proceeded to SIEGE CAMP. Two sections 7/198 M.G Company took over accommodation at KEMPTON PARK. One days Rations were serving to 374 sections.	
	9.	10 PM	No 374 section relieved in line by two sections of 198 M.G. Coy. proceeded from KEMPTON PARK to SIEGE CAMP in motor lorries. Relief complete.	
SIEGE CAMP	10.	9am 11.30am	Nos 1 & 2 section laid duckboard tracks in Camps. No 374 section and attached men from 2/5 London Regt. Laid gun approaches etc unexpected.	
	11.	9.30 K 11 P.M 11/12 Am	Inspection of Clothing small kit etc. Rknd was and Rifle Inspection	

A.534 Wt.W4973/M687. 750,000 8/16 D. D. & L. Ltd. Forms/C.2118/13.

WAR DIARY
or
INTELLIGENCE SUMMARY.

(Erase heading not required.)

Army Form C. 2118.

Instructions regarding War Diaries and Intelligence Summaries are contained in F. S. Regs., Part II. and the Staff Manual respectively. Title pages will be prepared in manuscript.

Place	Date Nov.	Hour	Summary of Events and Information	Remarks and references to Appendices
SIPER CAMP	12	9/30 11.30 AM	Cleaning Guns, Cleaning and repacking Kitchen	AJJ
"	13	9.30 AM 10.15 AM 11.15 AM 2/3 PM	Inspection by Section Officers. Inspection of Gas Helmets etc by Bde Gas Officer. Inspection of Belt refilling same in huts.	AJJ
"	14	10/30 AM 1 PM	Transport proceeds by road to PONT CAMP in PROVEN area Company Gas transport mules to ELVERDINGE STATION and in hand, detraining at PROVEN STATION and marching to PONT CAMP about one mile distant, arrived 6 P.M.	AJJ
PONT CAMP	15	9/30 A 10/30 10/30 11/30 11/30 2 PM	Stripping and assembling Mechanism. Gas Drill. Pay order of Company.	AJJ
"	16	9/30 AM 11/30	Cleaning and cleaning spare parts. Cleaning Vickers Mgy cleaning limbers and greasing, Repairing limbers. 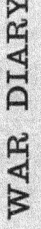	AJJ

WAR DIARY or INTELLIGENCE SUMMARY

Army Form C. 2118.

Place	Date Nov	Hour	Summary of Events and Information	Remarks and references to Appendices
Portland	17	9/30 to 11/30 2/30 to 4/30	Stripping & assembling. 10/30 to 11/30. Immediate Action. 11/30 to 11/30. Indication of Targets and sight setting & laying etc.	904
	18	11.15 AM 4.30 PM	Church Parade. C. of E. Bath for half company	1894
	19	7.45 AM	Numbers 3 & 4 section and remainder of transport paraded for baths. 11/30 to 12/30 PM. Squad drill and saluting drill for nos 3 & 4 sections. No 1 & 2 sections aid the following parades during this day. 9/30 to 10/30 Section inspected by section officers. Squad drill and saluting drill. 10/30 to 11/30 AM. Elementary Gun Drill 11/30 to 12/30 PM description of targets & laying.	904
	20	9/45	Physical Training 10 to 11 AM. Immediate Action 11/6 12 Noon Stopping and pain to Before cleaning & and after firing. 2/30 to 4 PM. Football Match 215 M.g. v 175 B.H.Q. 215 MG v 11 goals. 175 B.H.Q. Nil.	192
	21	9/45	Physical Training 10 to 11. Elementary drill 11/6 12 Noon. North section instruction in Anti Aircraft sights. Advanced party 1 Or 2 O.R. proceeded on cycles to new area.	1894

WAR DIARY
or
INTELLIGENCE SUMMARY

Army Form C. 2118.

Place	Date Nov	Hour	Summary of Events and Information	Remarks and references to Appendices
PONT CAMP	22nd	9/6/10	Inspection by Section Officers & immediate action Mechanism. "b" rt all section officers disposal	APX
		1 PM	Pay out of Company	
		2 PM	Section Officers Inspection Immediate action Mechanism "I/r" Stripping and description of spare parts	APX
do.	23.	9/6/10	Section Officers Inspection Immediate action Mechanism "I/r" Stripping and description of spare parts	APX
		10/11	pub: NCO's Inspection of Belts. F Tel at following times 9am Transport. 9.30 No. 1 & 2 Sections 10am No. 3 & 4 Sections. Remainder of day in town economy	APX
	24.			
	25.	10/30 AM	Church Parade C of E	APX
	26.	7.30 AM	Transport proceeds by march route to AFFRINGUES Physical Training 10 - 11 except Orr & Commission Duce Sections at Section Commanders disposal	APX
		9.6 gus		
		11.6 n		
	27	8.30 AM	Transport having been hitched for night 26/27 at ST HOMELIN proceeds to AFFRINGUES. The Company two transport marched to PROVEN STATION and entrained arriving WIZERNES 4.35 PM	APX
		10.74M		

Army Form C. 2118.

WAR DIARY
or
INTELLIGENCE SUMMARY.
(Erase heading not required.)

Instructions regarding War Diaries and Intelligence Summaries are contained in F. S. Regs., Part II. and the Staff Manual respectively. Title pages will be prepared in manuscript.

Place	Date Nov.	Hour	Summary of Events and Information	Remarks and references to Appendices
	27	4:30 PM	The Company marched into billets at AFFRINGUES at 5 PM.	28A
AFFRINGUES	28	9:30 AM	Repacking limbers & settling into billets.	28A
"	29	9 am	Sections inspected by Section Officers.	28A
		9:15 & 10	Gun Drill: 10 to 11 am Gun Drill 11.15 to Noon Gun Drill, 12 to 7 PM Gun and Clothing.	
	30	10/45 AM	Company marched to billets at AFFRINGUES and proceeded to KART, about 1 mile distant where gun drills were taken over.	28A

G. J. Hilton, Lt. M.G.
O.C.

215 MACHINE GUN COMPANY.

Army Form C. 2118.

215 - M G Coy
Vol 10

WAR DIARY
or
INTELLIGENCE SUMMARY.
(Erase heading not required.)

Instructions regarding War Diaries and Intelligence Summaries are contained in F.S. Regs., Part II. and the Staff Manual respectively. Title pages will be prepared in manuscript.

Place	Date	Hour	Summary of Events and Information	Remarks and references to Appendices
LART	1917 Dec 1	9.0-11.30 AM	Cleaning & preparing limbers. Remainder of day — washing, underclothing, repair of kits	fine
"	2	5.0-12.0	Bath at SENINGHEM Church Parade. Monsignor Prothyman at 12 noon in Relichnam at AFFRINGUES	
"	3	9.0-12.30	Route march	wet
"	4	9.15	Inspection by Section Officers	
		9.30-12.0	Army in Range	
			Lecture at Range	
"	5	9.0-9.30	Physical Drill	
		9.45-10.15	Lecture House Inspection. Inspection of Gas Helmets	
		10.15-11.15	Gun Drill	
		11.30-12.30	Lewis Drill	
		1.0	Advance party proceed by lorry to new area	
		6.30	Transport proceed by road to new area	fine
"	6	3.45 am	Company marched off. Proceeded by route march to LUMBRES where they Entrained and proceeded to WIZERNES station. Entrained at 7.30 am. Detrained at ELVERDINGHE and marched to SIEGE CAMP where huts were occupied. Transport having arrived at ST MOMELIN for the nap+ 5/6 proceed at 8.30 am into the ordered stage of journey.	
SIEGE CAMP	7	9.30-10.30	Gas alarm	
		10.30	Enemy action made one Pole morning for A.A. purposes	
			The transport having been billeted at ST JAN TER BIEZEN for night of 6/7 proceeded on that stage of journey arriving at SIEGE CAMP at 2.0 pm	
		2.30 pm	Lectures detailed Guns & Spare parts	

A.S.834 Wt.W4973/M687 750,000 8/16 D.D.&L.Ltd. Forms/C.2118/13.

WAR DIARY or INTELLIGENCE SUMMARY

Army Form C. 2118.

Place	Date	Hour	Summary of Events and Information	Remarks and references to Appendices
SIEGE CAMP	1917 DEC 8.	9.30 am	The company Gun Transport proceeded to KEMPTON PARK. No 2 section into Proceeded by motor ack ammunition by train	
	9		No 1 & N sections relieved 3 sections of 105 M.G.Coy. whilst :-	
			No 1 Section 1 gun at NOBLES FARM	
			1 " " HELLES HOUSE	
			4 " " THE BREWERY	
			2 " " BANFF HOUSE	
			2 " " TRACAS FARM	
			4 " " gun line onto the left subsection in LANGE MARCHE Coy HQ at KEMPTON PARK	
IN THE LINE	9		Situation normal. LT HOLLAND relieved 2/LT LEE at THE BREWERY	
	10		Situation normal. 96 M.G. Coy relieved two guns of No 2 section at BANFE HOUSE and put in No & moved to TRACAS FARM	
	11		Situation normal. E.A active slight shelling of front areas	
	12	9.30 am	Enemy aeroplane brought down by gun in [?] at KEMPTON PARK	
	13		Company relieved by 188 M.G. Coy on the night and walker F/14 M.G.Coy on left subsection for complete guns [?] moved to CANAL BANK arriving at 10 pm. The day devoted to cleaning & refitting up	
CANAL BANK	14	1630 am	Company proceeded to ROUSSEL CAMP occupying hut nits. CAPT HD DREW RAMC to VIK. Transport remained at BRIDGE CAMP	

Army Form C. 2118.

WAR DIARY
or
INTELLIGENCE SUMMARY.
(Erase heading not required.)

Instructions regarding War Diaries and Intelligence Summaries are contained in F. S. Regs., Part II. and the Staff Manual respectively. Title pages will be prepared in manuscript.

Place	Date	Hour	Summary of Events and Information	Remarks and references to Appendices
ROUSSEL CAMP	Dec 15 1917	9.30	Inspection of Rifles	
		10.30	Lecture Officers Inspection	
		10.45–11.30	Squad Drill	
		11.30–12.30	Clothing, cleaning guns & gun equipment	
		3.0 pm	Pay out of Company	
	16	11.0	Inspection by C.O.	
		11.30–12.30	Inspection of Gas helmets & Gas Drill	
	17	9.0	Physical Training	
		9.15–10.0	Lecture Officers Inspection	
		10.0–11.0	Squad Drill at Gas helmets	
		11.0–12.0	Gun Drill	
		12.0–12.30	Case cleaning	
	18	9.0–9.15	Lecture Officers Inspection	
	19	9.15	Preparatory lecture as transport changes BRIDGE CAMP	
		9.0	Section moved to transport lines for belt filling	
	20	9.0–9.30	Physical Training	
		10.30	C.O's Inspection	
		11.0–12.0	Lecture on Refugee duties of Maxim Belts	
		12.0–12.30	Case cleaning	
	21	9.0–9.30	Physical morning	
		9.45	Officers Inspection	
		10.0–11.0	Inspection of Gas Helmets by Bde Gas N.C.O	
		11.0–12.0	Instruction of gas use against dismounted Scouts	

WAR DIARY
or
INTELLIGENCE SUMMARY.
(Erase heading not required.)

Army Form C. 2118.

Instructions regarding War Diaries and Intelligence Summaries are contained in F. S. Regs., Part II. and the Staff Manual respectively. Title pages will be prepared in manuscript.

Place	Date	Hour	Summary of Events and Information	Remarks and references to Appendices
ROUSSEL CAMP	1917 Dec 22	10.15 am	Camp and firm transport moved to billets at CANAL BANK. Transport remained at BRIDGE CAMP	
CANAL BANK	23	11.0 am	Company firm transport moved to KEMPTON PARK	
		2.0 pm	No 1 Pln Section and a section from the Companies of 206 M.G. Coy to the line.	
LINE	24	10.10 pm	Relieved guns. Light shelling on front line pickets. 1 gun knocked out THE BREWERY blown up by shell fire, replaced by gun from Section H.Q. No casualties.	
"	25		Situation quiet. Light shelling of trenches at night, no gun came to Section HQ.	
"	26		At 5.45pm the enemy put down heavy arty H.E. + shrapnel on our left, followed by light green + amber green + red + red + green shells, S.O.S gun rapid rates. We 4.50pm and artillery replied to S.O.S 4 guns from target rapid. Same as above in report at 8.15pm Enemy Inf active front line and front posts. Artillery normal except S.O.S as above.	
"	27	2.0 pm	4 other guns came relieved U guns in the line at PHEASANT TRENCH, ROSE HOUSE, DELTA HOUSE and FAVOURITE	
"		2.30	N.W. LESTER redoubt N.W. Section b/c POELCAPPELLE N.W. 3 " " GLOSTER + TRACAS No 2	
			Artillery normal, E.A. active generally quiet. L/Cpl ELLIOT wounded	
"	28		Situation quiet, enemy normal. Lights shelling of battery area but few not more. E.A. active	
"	29		Situation quiet. At 5.35pm S.O.S. call from division left was answered by our artillery. Enemy put down heavy barrage on our left posts. Otherwise little artillery activity	
			E.A. generally inactive. Three minnenwerfer observed.	
"	30		No hostile artillery much below normal and enemy activity somewhat slowed.	

WAR DIARY
or
INTELLIGENCE SUMMARY.
(Erase heading not required.)

Army Form C. 2118.

Place	Date	Hour	Summary of Events and Information	Remarks and references to Appendices
LINE	Dec 30 (17)	8.0 pm	Barrage on our left rising enemy front. Our artillery put a barrage on our left front with M.G. and T.M. cooperation. Enemy barrage came down at 8 1/2 pm and continued over the whole front of our left Division. Many rockets were put up by the enemy during the hour 8.0-9.0 pm without apparent result. The S.O.S. appeared to turn green.	
"	31	6.0 am	Our artillery put a barrage in response to an S.O.S. from the centre on our right Company relieved by 201 M.G. Coy. relief complete by 8.30 pm and company moved from 16 huts at normandy subway G6Y in CANAL BANK	

signature
O.C.
215 MACHINE GUN COMPANY.

WAR DIARY or INTELLIGENCE SUMMARY

Army Form C. 2118.

215 M.G. Coy

Place	Date 1918	Hour	Summary of Events and Information	Remarks and references to Appendices
CANAL BANK	Jan 1	9 am	1. Company paraded for inspection of clothing, boots etc. to meet the transport train for the purpose of cleaning harness.	
"	2.		Company baths	
	3.	8.40 am	12 new pr. section proceeded to Transport lines to clean harness. Remainder of Company under section officers.	
		10 am	Horse cleaning continued and lectures by section officers.	
	4.			
	5.		Marching order received & men to hand in surplus kits and stores reviewed by O.C.	
	6.	10/30 am	Company proceeded by light railway to HERZEELE. Arrived and went into billets. Occupied by 10th M.G.C. movements.	
HUITTERQUE	7.	9 am	Commanding Officer inspected billets. Inspection declared very satisfactory. Guns and equipment taken for cleaning. Nos 2.3 pr cleaning guns and gun equipment. Tour of Guard mounting changed from 4 pm to 9 am.	
	8.	9 am	Building of stables continued and painting of Limbers commenced. Guns and Equipment finished.	

Army Form C. 2118.

WAR DIARY
or
INTELLIGENCE SUMMARY.
(Erase heading not required.)

Instructions regarding War Diaries and Intelligence Summaries are contained in F. S. Regs., Part II. and the Staff Manual respectively. Title pages will be prepared in manuscript.

Place	Date 1916	Hour	Summary of Events and Information	Remarks and references to Appendices
Hunts*ville	9.	1 pm	Rehearsal of parade for presentation of medals by Corps commander to Lieutt Henries Pte 11 and Pte 20 Pte 3.7 Markoo reported to Staff Capt on ground at 10 am.	
do	10.		Company duties. Cyclists course still and practice.	
	11.	8 a.m.	Company proceeded to Brigade parade ground Brigade inspected by Corps commander and medals presented to Capt Benn Harries, M.C. and Pvtes Scholes. H.M. Conference held after inspection. C.O.'s and Adjutants by Brigade Commander. Subject Defence principles.	
	12.	9.30 a.m.	Guns and Gun Equipment Inspection of inspection held. Company paraded on parade by G.O.C. 175 Brigade	
	13.		Company engaged on usual preparing for transport inspection. Warning order to proceed to Newhaven received.	
	14.		Firing on 30 yards range was carried out rounds S.A.A. expended. 2/Lieut McDonald proceed in advance to New Hive. to obtain billets.	
	15.		Owning to train moving in which carried out Transport inspection cancelled. Orders for move received.	

Army Form C. 2118.

WAR DIARY
or
INTELLIGENCE SUMMARY.
(Erase heading not required.)

Instructions regarding War Diaries and Intelligence Summaries are contained in F. S. Regs., Part II. and the Staff Manual respectively. Title pages will be prepared in manuscript.

Place	Date 1918	Hour	Summary of Events and Information	Remarks and references to Appendices
HOUSTREA	March 16	8.30am	Kits & Rifles inspected for cleaning purposes and became limbers to be inspected had to parade empty. The suspects proceeded to inspection ground with limbers for the purpose of examining said kicks upon proceeding to inspection. Remainder of company firing on range. (Lewis) 16000 rounds fired	(Orig.)
	17	9.50 to 10.5.11 am	Belt filling	Gun Drill. (Regimental day) (Orig.)
	18.	9am	Company paraded for range work & owing to rain work had to be abandoned.	(Orig.)
	19.	9.10am	Kit Inspection 10.15 to 11am Belt filling 11 to 12 NOON Gun Cleaning and repacking limbers.	(Orig.)
	20.	10.00am	Company moved to new area. Transport moved off at 12.30 p.m. and remainder of Company moved off at 2.15 pm and proceeded to NORTHERN CAMP. PROVEN to await train B entraining. Company entrained at PROVEN at 6 p.m.	(Orig.)
	21.		Company detrained at VILLERS-BRETENEUX at 8.30am, and proceeded by route march to AUBIGNY arriving there 10.45am.	(Orig.)
AUBIGNY	22.	9.30 am	Sorting and cleaning limbers & settling into billets.	(Orig.)

Army Form C. 2118.

WAR DIARY
or
INTELLIGENCE SUMMARY.

(Erase heading not required.)

Instructions regarding War Diaries and Intelligence Summaries are contained in F. S. Regs., Part II. and the Staff Manual respectively. Title pages will be prepared in manuscript.

215 COMPANY
24.12.16
MACHINE GUN CORPS

Place	Date	Hour	Summary of Events and Information	Remarks and references to Appendices
RUBIGNY	Dec 23 1916	9/10 am 10 am	Close order Drill: Names Corporals under C.S.M. Continued M.G. Drill. 11 to 12 noon Immediate Action with and without stoppages. 12 to 12.30 Care and cleaning	93/-
	24.	9/10	Route order Drill	
		11 to Noon	Nos 1 & 2 section with rifles 10 to 11 Gun Drill & Saluting. 11 to Noon Mechanism and stoppages 12 to 12.30 Care and cleaning. 93/-	93/-
	25.	9 am	Insp: section by section by Section Officers. 9.30 to 10.30 S.B.R. inspected by Coy.	
			Gas Officer. 10.30 to 11.30 Close Order Drill. Saluting drill. Nos 3 & 4 section with Rifles. 11.30 to 12.30 Lewis Gunners Drill.	93/-
		2.30 pm	Company paid.	
	26.	4 to 6 pm	Route March. Dress Fighting order.	93/-
	27	12 Noon	Coy E Church parade at École du Cos Garons.	93/-
	28.	8.30 to 10.30	Company Athletics at CORBIE. 11 to Noon rough ground drill.	93/-
			12 to 12.30 Care and cleaning.	
	29.	9 to 3 pm	Firing on 30' range CORBIE.	93/-
	30.	1 to 10	Close Order Drill Nos 1 & 2 with Rifles. 10 to 10.30 Lewis Drill. 10.30 to 11 Exceptions	93/-
			& Target 11 to 12 rough ground drill. 12 to 12.30 care and cleaning.	
	31.	9 am	Rigid Hay Company Inspected T.A.B. by M.O. 2/10th Bn. Bedfordshire Regt. Company half picnic.	93/-

C.M. Walker Lieut MG
O.C. 215 MACHINE GUN COMPANY.

To 58th Division

From O.C. 215 M.G. Company

I enclose herewith War Diary of this Unit for the month of February 1918, please.

9-3-18

.... O.C.
215 MACHINE GUN COMPANY.

Army Form C. 2118.

WAR DIARY
or
INTELLIGENCE SUMMARY.
(Erase heading not required.)

Instructions regarding War Diaries and Intelligence Summaries are contained in F. S. Regs., Part II. and the Staff Manual respectively. Title pages will be prepared in manuscript.

Place	Date	Hour	Summary of Events and Information	Remarks and references to Appendices
AUBIGNY.	FEB. 1st	9 AM.	Left Half company inoculated. T.A.B. Right Half company lectured by Section Officers on the employment of Machine Guns both Tactically & Technically: Mechanism.	A.4
		3 PM.	Company paid.	
	2nd	9 am	Lectures by Section Officers on "Recent Operations" Maps, and general principles of Machine Gunnery.	B.4
		10.30 am & 12.30	Mechanism.	
	3rd	9.15 am	Church Parade 6 p.m.: One finder entered for Brigade competition. No prize gained.	C.4
	4th	9 am & 3 PM.	Firing practice on Long Range.	D.4
	5th	9.10 am	Tent Billing 10 to 11am Packing limbers 11 to 12 noon. Close Order Drill.	E.4
		8.45 AM.	Five limbers and one G.S. Wagon commenced journey by road to new Area.	
	6.	6.20 AM.	Remainder of transport proceeded to CORBIE STATION for entrainment at 9am:	F.4
		8.15 AM.	Company bus transport proceeded by march route to CORBIE STATION for entrainment at 11 am.	
		5 PM.	Company arrived in New Area and detrained at FLAVY-DE-MARTEL. Thence the company proceeded by bus to FRIERE CAMP where they were accommodated in huts.	
	7th	5 PM.	Company proceeded to relieve the 212th M.G. Coy in the line: Disposition of sections were as follows: Nos 1 & 3 section Front line No.2. Bois de VIEVILLE No.1 Sec Company H.Q. at FORT LIEZ, TRANSPORT LINES, BOIS DE HALLOT.	G.4

A 5834 Wt W4973/M687 750,000 8/16 D. D. & L. Ltd. Form/C.2118/13

WAR DIARY
or
INTELLIGENCE SUMMARY.
(Erase heading not required.)

Army Form C. 2118.

Place	Date	Hour	Summary of Events and Information	Remarks and references to Appendices
LIME.	FEB. 8.	2 AM.	Relief of 21 M.G. Coy. Complete.	
"	9.		Very quiet day. Nothing to report.	
"	10.		Very quiet. Positions of guns in Battle Zone sited; light shelling of FORT VENDEUIL. Enemy Air craft very active: 250 rounds expended.	
"	11.		Quiet day; Gun teams shown all gun emplacements in Battle Zone and positions sited in Switch Line.	
	12.		Quiet Day. Practice Gun Alarms at FORT LIEZ, nothing to report.	
	13.		Light shelling of FORT VENDEUIL and FORT LIEZ.	
	14.		Enemy Aircraft active; one of our Observation Balloons brought down in flames: 750 rounds fired. Enemy LIEZ 1000 rounds fired at.	
	15.		Very quiet day. Nothing to report.	
	16.		Practise manning of Battle Zone positions; light shelling of FORT LIEZ and RONCONETTE FARM about 12. Noon to 2. PM. Pte COLLETT wounded slightly.	
	17.		C.R.E. visited positions in Battle Zone together with D.M.G.O. to decide positions for concrete emplacements and mining Dugouts.	
	18.		Nothing to report.	
	19.		Nothing to report.	
	20.		Enemy M.G. fires bursts through the night otherwise everything very quiet.	

Army Form C. 2118.

WAR DIARY
or
INTELLIGENCE SUMMARY.
(Erase heading not required.)

Instructions regarding War Diaries and Intelligence Summaries are contained in F.S. Regs., Part II. and the Staff Manual respectively. Title pages will be prepared in manuscript.

Place	Date FEB.	Hour	Summary of Events and Information	Remarks and references to Appendices
LINE.	21		Very Quiet: one of our observations again brought down by E.A. 500 rounds fired by own M.G.	
	22.		Very Quiet day.	
	23.		Nothing to report: one Officer returns from U.K. one Officer to A.A. Course.	
	24.		Work carried out on improvements in battle zone; very quiet day.	
	25.		Company relieved in the line by 55th Brigade M.G. Company.	
	26.	3AM.	Relief complete.	
	27.	2:30PM	Company ready for night of 25-26 at FRIERE CAMP. Company moved by march route to MARIZELLE and were accommodated in huts.	
	28.		Settling into Billets. Repairing and cleaning guns equipment.	

..........O.C.
215 MACHINE GUN COMPANY.

www.ingramcontent.com/pod-product-compliance
Lightning Source LLC
Chambersburg PA
CBHW081449160426
43193CB00013B/2424